The *Woman's* Book *of* Confidence

Guided Journal

Meditations for Strength and Inspiration

Sue Patton Thoele

Conari Press

Cover Design: Elina Diaz
Layout & Design: Jessica Dacher

For permission requests, please contact the publisher at:
Mango Publishing Group
2850 S Douglas Road, 4th Floor
Coral Gables, FL 33134 USA
info@mango.bz

For special orders, quantity sales, course adoptions and corporate sales, please email the publisher at sales@mango.bz. For trade and wholesale sales, please contact Ingram Publisher Services at customer.service@ingramcontent.com or +1.800.509.4887.

The Woman's Book of Confidence Guided Journal: Meditations for Strength and Inspiration

ISBN: (print) 978-1-64250-421-7 (ebook) 978-1-64250-422-4
BISAC category code: SEL032000, SELF-HELP / Spiritual

Printed in the United States of America

Were you ever told to stop being silly when you fantasized and imagined as a child? Were your dreams endorsed and encouraged or were they scoffed at by the big people you looked up to? What about now? Are the people in your life, including yourself, supportive of your aspirations? Many of the hopes, desires, and dreams we had as children were indicators of the special gifts we brought into this life. If we have lost track of our dreams, we can reconnect with them now by encouraging ourselves to look back and explore them.

What make-believe did you revel in

when you were little?

Where did you go in your fantasy world?

What did you want to be when you grew up?

What attracted you to those careers?

Honor and listen to your
    dreams—*current* and past.

"How badly the child needs a mediator, someone who can understand both words—heart and intellect—and help bring them a little closer together."

—IRENE CLAREMONT DE CASTILLEJO

How can you translate your childhood
dreams into adult realities?

How conscious and awake are you?

Stop and take time to appreciate life's little wonders.

Invite your wonder-filled inner child out to play.

List some ways to do this.

Do you savor the current moment or squander it in anticipation or dread of tomorrow?

Allowing yourself to recall pleasant memories
  facilitates your healing and fosters forgiveness. In
a quiet alone time, or with a trusted friend, make
  a list of any times you remember being happy
or contented as a child.

Replay those minutes or hours. Savor them.
  Relive the feelings and give thanks for
the experiences.

Accentuate the positive in your background.

Create a new family myth.

"Light tomorrow with today!"

—ELIZABETH BARRETT BROWNING

"One thing that comes out of myths is that at the bottom of the abyss comes the voice of salvation. The black moment when the real message of transformation is going to come. At the darkest moment comes the light."

—JOSEPH CAMPBELL

Take a few moments to review some of your
family myths. Are they fact or fable?

Do they enhance your life or diminish it?

Does your self-esteem soar or suffer

in the light of these traditions?

Are these legacies that you want

to pass on to your children?

"And remember, we all stumble, every one of us.
That's why it's a comfort to go hand in hand."

—E.K. BROUGH

Many of us are afraid to take the risks that would see our dreams to fruition.

Do you have a dream? Is there an activity
in which you secretly long to participate?

One of the best ways to transform your fears
is to figure out whether or not they're realistic.

Are you avoiding an occupational risk because of fear?

Divide a sheet of paper into three columns labeled:
"My Dream" or "What I Would Like to Do"; "Fears
Inhibiting Me"; and "How I Can Transform These
Fears." Quickly jot down answers that come to you
under the appropriate column.

Encourage yourself to live your dreams. List some ideas that will help them manifest.

Accept risk as a part of doing business.

"To live is so startling it leaves little

time for anything else."

—EMILY DICKINSON

*Stop living in the mists
of "Someday I'll..."*

Do you take advantage of opportunity or

crouch fearfully in the shadows?

"You may be disappointed if you fail,

but you're doomed if you don't try."

—BEVERLY SILLS

Women are amazing

Our lives are rarely a straight trajectory; instead, we weave together an abundant existence from the varied and often unexpected occurrences that we encounter. Sociologists claim that women, because we are required to pay attention to many things at once, are multi-minded and have great tolerance for interruption. Anyone who has juggled motherhood, career, education, significant relationships, household management, and self-growth knows this to be true.

As we lay down the warp and woof of our lives, we also need to be sure we weave strong safety nets for ourselves. When demands on us exceed our energy, we need to know how to support ourselves in finding the rejuvenation necessary to continue to thrive.

There are many ways — such as learning to understand and honor our needs, having realistic expectations, asking for help, and abolishing guilt — by which we can weave a supportive safety net for ourselves.

"*Woman must not depend upon the protection of man, but must be taught to protect herself.*"

—SUSAN BROWNELL ANTHONY

Is your inner dialogue
overly critical?

You deserve to be spoken to in encouraging ways.

You have the power to change your critical inner voice to a loving and supportive one.

"When sleeping women wake, mountains move."

—CHINESE PROVERB

Encourage your body by listening to its wisdom.

What is your body telling you right now?

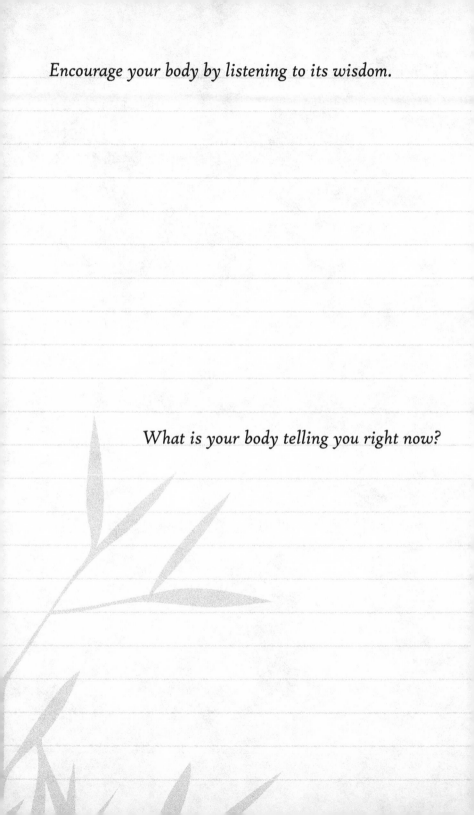

"We should not pretend to understand the world
    only by intellect; we apprehend
it just as much by feeling."

—CARL JUNG

"Guilt: the gift that keeps on giving."

—ERMA BOMBECK

Feeling guilty drains your confidence.

Do you want to keep feeling guilty about it?

Does this feeling and circumstance
remind you of a pattern in your family?

Write down what you feel guilty about.
Now, with the biggest, reddest marker you
can find, cross it out—delete it.

Worry is a habit that knocks the supports right out from under us. One of the most freeing changes you can make in your life is to kick the worry habit.

"*Anxiety is love's greatest killer, because it*
is like the stranglehold of the drowning."

—ANAÏS NIN

Believe that life is good.

"Worry often gives a small thing a big shadow."

—SWEDISH PROVERB

"If I could identify one core problem about the world, it's that we've been taught to distrust ourselves."

—SHAKTI GAWAIN

As we journey through life, we play many parts;
indeed, we seem to be entirely different people
at various ages. Take a moment to recount
some of the adventures your "different people"
have had at various stages in your life.

"As selfishness and complaint pervert and cloud the mind, so love with its joy clears and sharpens the vision."

—HELEN KELLER

"For peace of mind, resign as general manager of the universe."

—LARRY EISENBERG

Being a perfect person, having a perfect relationship, or doing all things perfectly—there ain't no such thing! Recognizing this increases our day-to-day happiness.

What does your inner perfectionist look like?

Why does she act the way she does?

What is she afraid of?

"*Where you tend a rose, my lad,*
    A thistle cannot grow."
— FRANCES HODGSON BURNETT

Loss in life is unavoidable, and descending into the grief of loss is, initially, a plunge into emotional hell. When racked with sorrow we simply need to survive, finding what comfort and solace we can from sources that nurture and sustain us. In order to heal naturally and grow through our pain, we must first allow ourselves to feel it.

In spite of the pain, grief can also be the doorway to the rich cavern of our being, the sanctuary of our soul. Growing through loss enables us to evolve into deeper levels of confidence and maturity. When we are committed to growth, we will, step by tiny step, make the arduous climb out of the pit of loss carrying the precious jewels of strength, resilience, and a greater capacity for empathy and caring.

"I like living. I have sometimes been wildly, despairingly, acutely miserable, racked with sorrow, but through it all I still know quite certainly that just to be alive is a grand thing."

—AGATHA CHRISTIE

"Sorrow is such a faithful guide."

—JAN ESHER

As an exercise in cradling yourself with comfort, close your eyes and place your hands over your heart. For a few quiet moments, concentrate on the rhythm of your heart. Give thanks for your heart's faithfulness. Allow to come into your mind's eye a picture of yourself when in pain. Compassionately observe the you who is hurting. Who is she?

What is she feeling?

Who is there who can comfort her?

What person or thing outside of her can cradle her
as she grieves?

We all need to be protected by friends
who can listen nonjudgmentally
and support us unconditionally.

"*A friend may well be reckoned
the masterpiece of Nature.*"
—RALPH WALDO EMERSON

*You are supportive of yourself
  and others when a painful door
needs opening.*

"*A woman's life can really be a succession of lives, each revolving around some emotionally compelling situation or challenge, and each marked off by some intense experience.*"

— WALLIS SIMPSON, THE DUCHESS OF WINDSOR

Like a nagging ache or pain, unfinished
business is enervating and discouraging.

Unfinished business can include things we
regret having said, kindnesses left undone,
muddied misunderstandings, or times
we wished we had stood up for ourselves.
Create a list of your unfinished business.

First, redo! If there is something you regret doing and
it's possible to redo it by taking a new,
different action, do so. What are your do-overs?

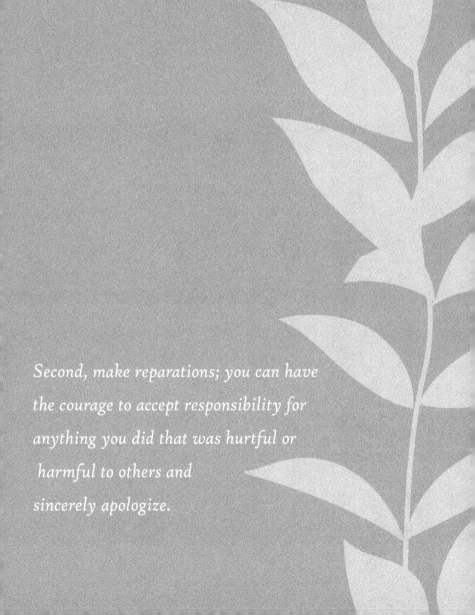

Second, make reparations; you can have the courage to accept responsibility for anything you did that was hurtful or harmful to others and sincerely apologize.

Third, it is important that you know when to
release your feelings about any injury you
have caused or sustained. How will you recognize
when it's time to let go?

You have the courage to
apologize for past mistakes.

"Fire destroys that which feeds it."

—SIMONE WEIL

Integrating anger into your life is crucially important to your sense of well-being. Much of women's depression is actually suppressed anger. How can you learn to tell the difference?

You deserve to be supported as you move through difficult feelings.

"*I find that it is not the circumstances in which we are placed, but the spirit in which we meet them that constitutes our comfort.*"

—ELIZABETH KING

*To love is to risk loss, but not to love
is to ensure emotional death.*

If you choose to really live, you will need to

        accept a certain amount of grief as well.

If we don't avail ourselves of emotional support
*   at difficult times, we run the risk of closing our*
hearts in order to escape sorrow. Who do you lean
*   on during difficult times?*

"It isn't for the moment you are stuck that you need courage, but for the long uphill climb back to sanity and faith and security."

— ANNE MORROW LINDBERGH

"The heart is the hub of all sacred places.

Go there and roam in it."

—SRI NITYANANDA

"We are all born to be a blessing."

—RACHEL NAOMI REMEN

A friend of mine attending a conference was surprised to notice that everyone at the breakfast table had coffee but her. She felt a little miffed and said, "Why didn't I get coffee?" Someone answered, "You have to turn your cup over, June, in order for them to pour you some." Isn't that what we often do—forget to turn our cup up to receive?

Why do we often have such qualms about anticipating and accepting abundance? Maybe it's because historically we women rendered services that were largely taken for granted—rather than respected and reimbursed—and we learned to give to others but not expect anything for ourselves. In order to invite abundance into our lives we need to feel worthy of the myriad blessings life has to offer: supportive relationships, peace of mind, well-balanced kids, health, enough money, and satisfying work.

Whatever the reasons for our hesitancy in accepting all forms of prosperity into our lives, it is important now that we change any limiting beliefs and awaken to the realization that we deserve to live abundant lives both practically and emotionally.

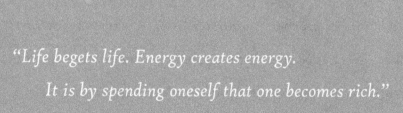

"*Life begets life. Energy creates energy.*
    It is by spending oneself that one becomes rich."
— SARAH BERNHARDT

You can choose what you look at, listen to,
and respond to—and reframe your reality.

Quietly think of a situation in your life
   that you consider difficult or depressing.
Describe it here.

Think about how you're framing the situation.

Are you making it unnecessarily dark or heavy?

Are you enlarging it beyond a reasonable size?

How would you like to frame this situation?

Allow a new frame to appear, one more manageable and maybe even beautiful. What change in attitude will you need in order to reframe your picture?

When this situation next arises, take a moment

to see it in the context of your new frame.

You can choose to see
    how wonderful your life is.

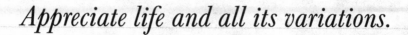

Appreciate life and all its variations.

"What a wonderful life I've had.

I only wish I'd realized it sooner."

— SIDONIE-GABRIELLE COLETTE

"Hope is the feeling you have that

    the feeling you have isn't permanent."

—JEAN KERR

In the face of uncomfortable circumstances, sometimes the only thing you have the power to change is your mind. How often do you utilize that power?

Knowing you are in charge of your attitudes
is one of the most life-enhancing
realizations you can come to.

Be proud of being an optimist.

*Because we are sentenced to the consequences
of our accumulated thoughts, it is important that
we learn to observe and elevate them. Write out
some negative thoughts you commonly have and
practice elevating them to positive thoughts.*

"*It is not possible for the human mind to
    hold both a positive and a negative thought
at the same time.*"

— LILY TOMLIN

As an exercise in helping you observe and elevate your thoughts, imagine that everyone can read your mind. When a negative thought comes into your mind that you would rather keep to yourself, acknowledge it non-judgmentally and then replace it with an uplifting one.

"The last of the human freedoms is to choose one's attitude in any given set of circumstances."

—VIKTOR FRANKL

"*Peace and love are alive in us, but we are not always alive in peace and love.*"

—JULIAN OF NORWICH

Sometimes, your attitudes and beliefs about abundance launch you into the river of life and cause you to struggle upstream. Practicing gratitude will often help lighten your load. What are you grateful for?

When you believe that you are worthy to receive and that the universe benevolently wishes to give to you, you can flow with the stream of abundance and feel well cared for and wealthy no matter what the circumstances.

"Gratitude is heaven itself."

— WILLIAM BLAKE

Relationships are as important to us women as the very air we breathe. Without relationships we feel bereft, cut off from vital sources of comfort and support. Yet, with our busy schedules, have we been able to make it a priority to keep our relationships current? Luckily, most of our heart-held relationships, those that add to our lives and multiply our blessings, are fairly drought-resistant and can thrive on bursts of concentrated love and attention. But if nurturing and sustaining our relationships feels like yet another energy-draining obligation, we need to change our perception and see friendship as a sacred, life-enhancing gift we give and receive.

Elizabeth Yates wrote a beautiful passage in her book Up the Golden Stair: "Keep your relationships current. Follow the impulse to do that small kindness for another whenever it comes to you. Then you will never be beset by the thought, Oh, if I had only done it when I thought of it—This is one of the discoveries I have made this year: that if the inner promptings of heart and mind are obeyed there will never be an echo of the words 'too late.'"

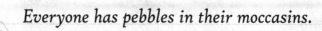

Everyone has pebbles in their moccasins.

In order to understand someone else we
need to walk in their shoes—exchange our
point of view for theirs—for a little while.

"Even a small thorn causes pain."

—IRISH PROVERB

If you feel lost in a labyrinth of other people's demands and desires, try unearthing any unhealthy fears or beliefs you have that are allowing you to be taken for granted. Write them here.

To help yourself discover areas where you disappear
into availability, write a list of circumstances
in which you feel used or taken for granted.

For each separate entry ask yourself why you continue to act in a way that results in your feeling invisible and undervalued.

Question your fear: Is it realistic?

Is this an old fear from childhood that has no validity in your current life?

Who, in your inner cast of characters,
is experiencing the fear?

What do they need from you to help alleviate their fear? If your fear is realistic, what is the worst thing that could happen if you changed your behavior?

*Do you have the maturity and wisdom
to support yourself emotionally if the
worst scenario was realized?*

*Healthy availability enhances
relationships, but self-denial and
overindulgence destroy them.*

"*If you don't like what's happening in your life, change your mind.*"

—HIS HOLINESS THE DALAI LAMA

"*It is not because angels are holier than men or devils that makes them angels, but because they do not expect holiness from another, but from God alone.*"

—WILLIAM BLAKE

Mango Publishing, established in 2014, publishes an eclectic list of books by diverse authors—both new and established voices—on topics ranging from business, personal growth, women's empowerment, LGBTQ studies, health, and spirituality to history, popular culture, time management, decluttering, lifestyle, mental wellness, aging, and sustainable living. We were recently named 2019 and 2020's #1 fastest-growing independent publisher by *Publishers Weekly*. Our success is driven by our main goal, which is to publish high-quality books that will entertain readers as well as make a positive difference in their lives.

Our readers are our most important resource; we value your input, suggestions, and ideas. We'd love to hear from you—after all, we are publishing books for you!

Please stay in touch with us and follow us at:
 Facebook: Mango Publishing
 Twitter: @MangoPublishing
 Instagram: @MangoPublishing
 LinkedIn: Mango Publishing
 Pinterest: Mango Publishing
 Newsletter: mangopublishinggroup.com/newsletter

Join us on Mango's journey to reinvent publishing, one book at a time.